So Many Ways to Be Curious

A book to nurture curiosity,
critical thinking skills,
empathy and resilience

by Jayneen Sanders   illustrated by Clare Elsom

So Many Ways to Be Curious

Educate2Empower Publishing an imprint of
UpLoad Publishing Pty Ltd
Victoria Australia
www.upload.com.au

First published in 2025
Text copyright © Jayneen Sanders 2025
Illustration copyright © UpLoad Publishing Pty Ltd 2025

Written by Jayneen Sanders
Illustrations by Clare Elsom

Jayneen Sanders asserts her right to be identified as the author of this work.
Clare Elsom asserts her right to be identified as the illustrator of this work.

Designed by Jo Hunt

ISBN: 9781761160547 (hbk) 9781761160530 (pbk)

A catalogue record for this
book is available from the
National Library of Australia

'The more questions you ask,
the more questions you create!'

J. S.

Humans have always been **curious**. That's why nothing stays the same. People work out new ways of looking at old problems and **invent**, **create** and **wonder**, 'What if?'.

I hope this book encourages you to look at things from many points of view, and to always be curious!

Questions!

Curious people ask a **zillion** questions!

Why don't you ask an older person seven questions?

Each question should start with WHO? WHEN? WHAT? WHY? HOW? WHICH? WHERE?

Did you know!

Babies are born curious. During a baby's first year of life their brain will double in size. They will learn what a smile means, how to roll over, and that crying is a good way to get someone to notice them.

Listening to Others' Points of View

Listening to others' points of view and experiences is a way to be **curious**. For example, maybe you like chocolate ice cream but your friend likes lemon sorbet. You might ask them why they like lemon sorbet. And instead of thinking chocolate ice cream is the best — be **curious**: try lemon sorbet next time and make up your own mind. Encourage your friend to do the same. Be **curious** about all the flavors and maybe, over time, try them all!

What is a new ice cream flavor you'd like to TRY?

What is something else you'd like to TRY but never have?

Mindfulness

Curious people are also **mindful**. Mindfulness means you are fully present in the moment. You are not thinking about the future or the past, but you are paying attention to where you are now. For example, you might be going through a forest and instead of rushing to get to the end of the trail, take your time to be where you are.

Slow down and look around. Use all your senses that are available to you. **Listen** to the wind in the trees and the birds singing above you.

Describe what you can
SEE, SMELL, TOUCH, HEAR
or TASTE right now.

Breathe in the fresh forest air and smell the damp earth. Notice the different types of creatures around you. Spot the largest tree to the tiniest bugs along the trail. Maybe lie back in a clearing and watch the cloud shapes roll across the sky or touch the raindrops sparkling on the leaves.

There will always be so much to discover if you take the time to wonder and be curious.

Empathy

Curiosity helps you to be empathic. **Empathy** means you try your best to understand what another person or living creature is feeling. To have **empathy** you need to be **curious**. You need to **wonder** what it's like for another and ask questions. For example, you might ask how the person is feeling, why might they be feeling that way, and if there is anything you can do to help. It is important to listen with **curiosity** and **understanding**.

FRIENDSHIP BENCH

When have you shown EMPATHY to another person or a pet?

Problem Solve

Curious people love to solve problems. They love to work out a way to fix or manage a tricky problem. For example, maybe you need to move a heavy object from one end of the school to the other.

FLOUR 50

A **curious** person will keep on trying different ways until the problem is solved. When a person tries, and keeps on trying, we say they are **resilient**.

FLOUR 50

How are you RESILIENT?
What problems have you SOLVED?

Question What You Hear

Being **curious** means you don't always believe what you are told. You have a voice, and you have the right to ask as many question as you like. For example, if your teacher says the earth is round, say, **'How do you know?'** Keep asking questions. Keep being **curious** until you have found out all you want to know.

Just imagine if people believed everything they are told, and they never questioned any of it. If that were the case, we would still believe the earth was flat!

Scientists and engineers are some of the most **curious** people on the planet, and thank goodness they are. Their **curious** minds help us and our earth home every single day.

High speed shaft

Generator

Rotar hub

2x

$C \times m\sqrt{b}$

Can you think of some WAYS that scientists and engineers HELP us and our planet?

Choice

Curious people make their own choices. They might choose to try new foods, explore other countries and cultures, learn the piano or paint pictures of only orange and green. They might like to do or find out about all sorts of things — because they have choice, and they are curious.

What kind of CHOICES do you make for yourself?

Explore

Curious people love to **explore** new places and new ideas. They might **explore** parks, nature trails, mountains, beaches and rivers. But they might also **explore** libraries, museums, art galleries, theatre performances, research papers, newspapers and the Internet.

There is so much to **explore** and learn in our world, and there are so many places to **explore!**

RAINFORESTS

SUNSHINE

DRAGON

Where is your favorite place to EXPLORE?

Interests

Curious people may follow lots of interests or only one. They might try lots of new hobbies or just focus on one and find out everything there is to know about that hobby. They may become so passionate about what they are interested in that they become an expert. For example, you might love dinosaurs, so you find out all you can about dinosaurs and become an absolute expert! How cool would that be!

What are you really really INTERESTED in?

An 8-year-old Australian girl, Emma Glenfield, was curious why a magpie in her school yard (Mr Swoopsalot) only swooped tall, bald-headed men. So, she designed a survey that went viral and collected 30,000 responses from across the world. The results of her research have become very useful to Australian scientists.

Emma also keeps a journal full of questions. She writes down a question when one comes into her mind. She doesn't always answer it, but it keeps her curious about the world. What a fantastic idea!

MAGPIE SURVEY

Would you like to keep a journal and fill it with QUESTIONS that pop into your mind?

Imagination

Curious people are imaginative. They create new ways of seeing things and imagine all kinds of worlds through stories, music and art. For example, a curious person might imagine a world where there are weird and strange creatures living in a place that is very different to our earth. They might use these imaginings to create stories, pictures and music. Being curious encourages you to wonder and to imagine a new way of seeing.

Describe the strangest world you can IMAGINE.

Willing to Be Wrong

Curious people are willing to be wrong. They listen to others' points of view and the facts presented to them, and are willing to change their mind. For example, you might believe that emus can fly. But with some research, you find out you were wrong; and in fact, emus can't fly.

What have you gotten WRONG?

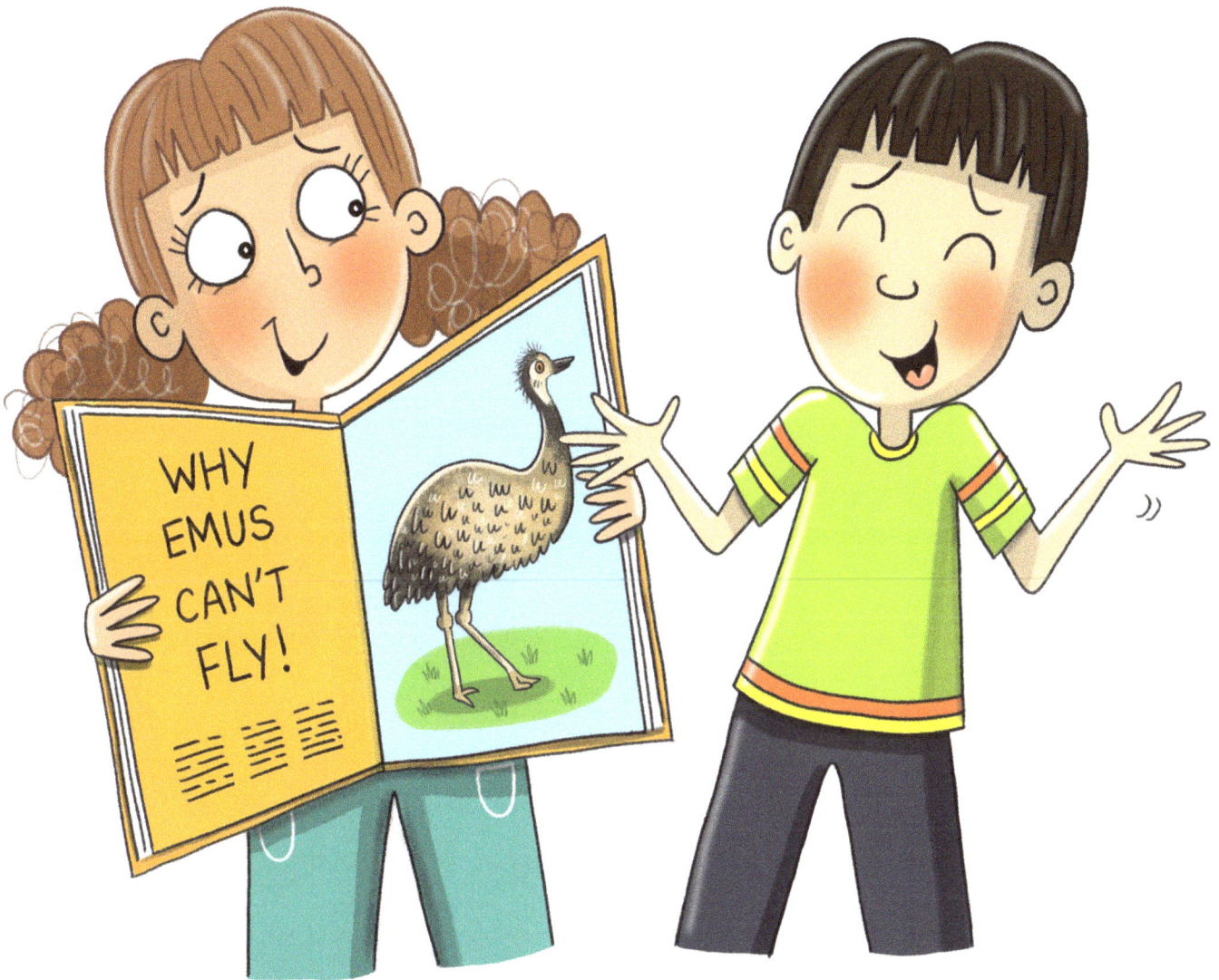

WHY EMUS CAN'T FLY!

A **curious** person will be able to happily admit that they got something wrong. Being able to admit you are **wrong** can stop an argument before it begins.

Disagree Respectfully

You may not always agree with everyone's ideas and points of view, and that's okay. **Curious** people will always **listen** with interest to others' points of view and when they don't agree, they **disagree respectfully**.

For example, you may think dogs are the best pets, but your friend thinks cats make much better pets. There is no need for an argument — a **curious** person will **listen** to their friend's ideas, and then put their point of view across and the reasons behind it. It's perfectly okay to agree to disagree — as long you do it **respectfully!**

Which do you think makes the best pets — dogs or cats?

Why do you say that?

What does RESPECTFULLY mean?

Interested in Other People's Stories

Curious people are interested in other people's **stories**, **cultures** and **way of life**. They love to learn about different foods, dress, festivals, beliefs and more. They are **interested** in people's abilities and how they live their life. They ask lots of **questions** and **listen** carefully to the answers. And most importantly, they do not judge a person if they live differently to them.

How do you show you are a good LISTENER?

MENU

Never ever stop being **curious**. Even as you get older. Always have an open mind to all kinds of possibilities.

Wondering, learning, exploring, questioning, discovering, problem solving
— all these skills equal **curiosity**.

Our world needs **curious** people more than ever because our planet is changing. Your **curiosity** will make this world a better place for all.

WE NEED CHANGE

In what kinds of ways are you CURIOUS?

Curious people:

imagine

create

learn

invent

explore

discover

listen

play

problem solve

investigate

ask questions

wonder

hypothesize

Curious people are:

inquisitive

empathetic

resilient

listen without judgment

observant

able to disagree respectfully

playful

fully present

open-minded

mindful

willing to be wrong

Ideas to Encourage Curiosity

- Visit a park, farm, nature reserve and/or the beach with your child, and encourage them to explore, wander and wonder! Allow them the space and time to investigate at their own pace, e.g. climb trees, collect pebbles or shells, explore rock pools, make 'fairy houses', play in the mud, splash in the puddles, or look for interesting insects and plants.

- Provide various colored paints and have your child paint pictures of any color. They could even use their hands to paint. Maybe provide different textured materials and have them use these to make prints on paper. Use playdough or clay and encourage your child to explore these materials with their hands. They may wish to make something or not. They might just like to squish the clay between their fingers!

- Make up a set of cards with open-ended questions for which there is no simple 'yes' or 'no' answer, e.g. 'What is your favorite color and why? What does red mean to you? What would you do if you didn't have to go to school?' Devise the cards to suit the age of your child.

- Encourage your child to carry our experiments and/or research. Ask them what they would like to research or what experiments interest them. If they don't have any ideas, visit the library and take out a book on experiments. Your child might also like to experiment with you in the kitchen with new recipes.

- If you have the space, make a vegetable garden together. Find out what the different plants need in order to grow, i.e. position for sunlight, water, fertilizer, etc. If you don't have space, grow some herbs in pots and use these in new recipes.

- Encourage your child's curiosity around anything that interests them. For example, they may love dogs. Encourage them to find out everything about dogs, i.e. breeds, best food for dogs, working dogs, training a dog, etc. If you intend for your child to get a pet, ensure they have learnt as much as possible about its needs.

- Have your child interview an older relative or friend to find out about their life and especially their childhood. Encourage your child to devise a list of general questions to ask. Have them practice asking these questions with you to fine tune their interviewing skills, i.e. looking the person in the eye when chatting, nodding to show interest, encouraging phrases your child can use to ensure the interviewee continues their story.

- Read books with your child and then have an informal discussion about the content. For example, you might read *The Giving Tree* by Shel Silverstein together. Have some questions ready about the story, e.g. 'How might the boy/ tree be feeling? Why do you say that? Do you think the boy/tree is kind? Why do you think that?' Ensure you answer the questions too. Model conversational skills throughout the discussion such as, 'I understand what you are saying but I think…' Model that listening to another's opinion is very important and often there are no right or wrong answers when it comes to people's opinions.

- Have your child use all the senses available to them to describe what they can hear, see, smell, touch or taste in this moment. Model an example: 'I can hear the trucks on the road. Their wheels are making swishy sounds as they travel over the wet road.' You can also ask questions which will encourage them to elaborate, e.g. say, 'You can smell lavender in the garden. Where else have you smelt lavender? What did you enjoy the most at the lavender farm?'

- Model curiosity yourself and enthusiasm for your child's curiosity. Learn together.

- Encourage the art of 'conversation' by modeling listening skills, questioning techniques, eye contact, presenting differing points of view, etc.

Discussion Questions
for Parents, Caregivers and Educators

The following Discussion Questions are a guide only. They can be used to open up discussions with your child around curiosity, mindfulness, resilience and empathy. *So Many Ways to Be Curious* can be read in one sitting or over several sittings.

Pages 4–5
Ask, 'What does invent/create/wonder mean? Do you think you are a curious person? Why do you say that?' Discuss what the characters on the page are doing. Ask, 'What was the problem? And what have these children created to solve that problem?'

Pages 6–7
Ask, 'Why do you think it is important to ask questions?' Have your child ask an older adult (or you) the questions as per page 7. Swap roles. If your child is interested, you could have them research other things babies learn and how our brains develop. Note: the question word 'which' refers to more specific information, e.g. 'Which color do you like: red or blue?'

Pages 8–9
The objective of this spread is for children to develop and open mind from a young age. It encourages them to listen to new information with curiosity and not to be rigid in their ideas and thought patterns. Ask more generic questions once you have discussed ice cream flavors, e.g. 'What is your favorite game? Why do you like that game?' Encourage your child to now ask you what your favorite game is. Model a response like, 'My favorite game is Uno, but I am willing to try your favorite game to see if I like it better.'

Pages 10–11
Encourage your child to wander and wonder! Mindfulness and being fully present in the moment help us to be curious about our environment. Go to a forest, park or to the beach and practice 'tuning in' with your child to all the senses available to them. Ask, 'What are you feeling/seeing/smelling/hearing, etc.?' From this excursion, other forms of curiosity may emerge such as writing about what was seen, painting a picture, or further research into what was discovered. Ask, 'What do you think the notice board on page 10 is used for?'

Pages 12–13
Unpack the meaning of 'empathy' with your child. Ask, 'When have you shown empathy towards another person or animal? Do you think a bully shows empathy? Why/Why not? If another child looks sad and alone, what could you do? Do you have a friendship bench at school? How is the child, sitting to the right of the bench, showing curiosity/empathy? What might be wrong with the dog on page 13? How are the children showing empathy?'

Pages 14–15
Ask, 'Do you like problem solving? What problems have you solved? What kind of problems could we solve? Do they always have to be about maths or science? Could we solve problems that we might be having

with friends and family? How might we solve that kind of problem? What do you think resilient means? Is it okay to make mistakes? Why do you say that? What have you learnt from making mistakes?' Remind your child that they might not be able to solve a problem yet; emphasize 'yet'.

Pages 16–17
Ask, 'Do you ask lots of questions of the grown-ups in your life? What do you think scientists and engineers do?' Your child might like to research exactly what scientists and engineers do, and how they help our planet.

Pages 18–19
Ask, 'What choices do you make? Are there any new foods you have tried or would like to try? What countries/cultures would you like to find out about? What is something new you'd like to learn to do?' Encourage your child in daily life to make as many of their own choices as possible.

Pages 20–21
Ask, 'What places do you like to explore? Where is your favorite place to explore?' Encourage the physical exploration of libraries, museums, art galleries, etc. as places of curiosity. Explain that the people whose works are featured must have been curious too!

Pages 22–23
Encourage your child to follow their interests. You could suggest they create a project using any medium they would like and present it to their class or family.

Pages 24–25
Encourage your child's imagination by reading them imaginative stories and showing them art featuring 'imagined'

places. Encourage your child to notice shapes in the clouds. Play a game of 'What is that cloud?' Have your child write, draw or describe the strangest world they can imagine.

Pages 26–27
Willing to be wrong is a key skill for everyone. Model this with your child and model listening to other points of view and/or new information. Ask, 'When did you get something wrong? Where you able to happily admit your mistake? Why do you think it is important to say you got something wrong?'

Pages 28–29
Everyone has the right to disagree with another's point of view, but we need to point out that disagreements can, and should, be respectful. Ask, 'How might you disagree with someone respectfully?' Model phrases such as, 'I hear what you are saying, but I think…I actually disagree with you, and these are my reasons why…' Reinforce that we don't necessarily have to say, 'I'm sorry' (women, in particular, say sorry far too often) but put our point of view across respectfully.

Pages 30–33
Expand your child's understanding of differing cultures by going to festivals and cultural displays and/or exploring various ways of life in books and films. Encourage your child to include all children of all abilities in their play and conversations. Ask, 'How will curiosity make our world a better place? How is each child on pages 32 and 33 showing curiosity?'

Pages 34–35
Unpack the meaning of the words and phrases with your child.

Books by the Same Author

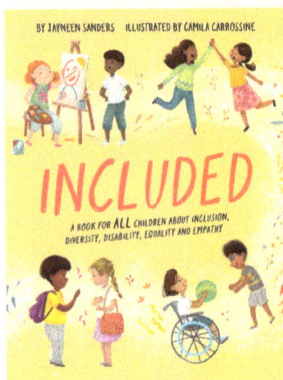

Included

Meet six wonderful kids! They love playing games and being silly. And just like kids everywhere they want to feel safe, loved and included. This book explores diversity and inclusion, and helps ALL kids understand that kids with disability are just like kids everywhere.

Discussion Questions included.
Ages 4 to 12 years

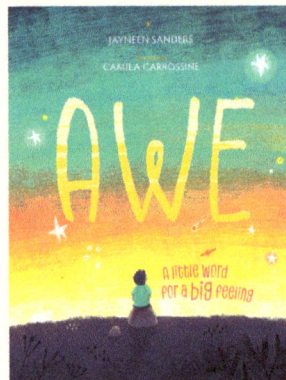

AWE

Awe increases our joy and sense of wonder. It encourages gratefulness, and helps us to understand that the world is so much bigger than ourselves. This beautifully illustrated book celebrates the beauty that surrounds us — we just need to take the time to notice.

Ages 5 to 11 years.

Everyone's Invited!

Using bright and colorful illustrations and written using rhythm and rhyme, this fun and inclusive book will ensure all children know that they matter.

Discussion Questions included.
Ages 4 to 9 years.

Be the Difference

This engaging book provides over 40 powerful ideas on how kids can make a difference. It focuses on three key areas: empathy and kindness, racial and gender equality, and the environment.

Discussion Questions included.
Ages 5 to 12 years.

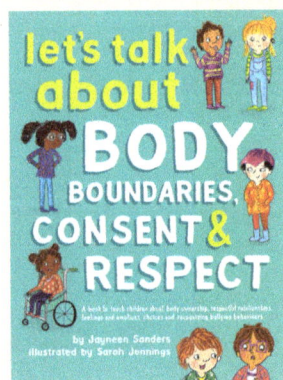

Let's Talk About Body Boundaries, Consent and Respect

Through familiar scenarios, this book opens up crucial conversations with children around consent and respect.

Discussion Questions included.
Ages 4 to 10 years.

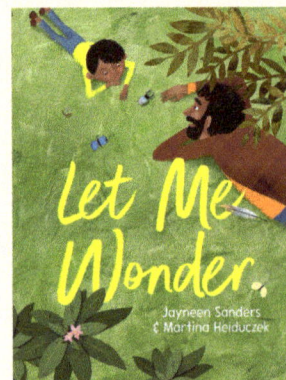

Let Me Wonder

Using rhythm and rhyme and stunning illustrations, this book explores the importance of play, connection and being fully present with the people around us and the environment in which we live.

Ages 3 to 10 years.

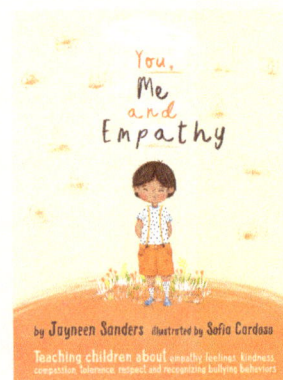

You, Me and Empathy

This charming story uses verse, beautiful illustrations and a little person called Quinn to model the meaning of empathy, kindness and compassion.

Discussion Questions and activities to promote empathy and kindness included.
Ages 3 to 9 years.

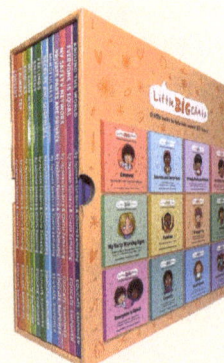

Little Big Chats series

This series has been written to help parents, carers and educators initiate age-appropriate conversations with early learners around crucial, and yet at times, 'tough' topics such as body safety, gender equality and diversity.

Discussion Questions included.
Ages 2 to 6 years.

For more information go to: www.e2epublishing.info

www.ingramcontent.com/pod-product-compliance
Lightning Source LLC
Chambersburg PA
CBHW041636040426
42448CB00023B/3491